NELSON MANDELA LEGACY

A Nelson Mandela Biography

Michael Woodford

Table of Contents

A Historical Perspective

There are 11 official languages in South Africa. It is among the most diverse nations in the world. The story of how this land was settled and claimed throughout the centuries is a vast and complicated study.

Instead, the objective here is to consider the life of one of the most important South Africans to ever live. But his was a fame and influence that stretched much farther than his country's borders. South Africa needed a voice for the world to care, he was that voice. He was Nelson Mandela.

So much has been written about his life and many more will write about his spirit, far into the future. The only hope of a simple biography, such as this one, is to scratch the surface of what made him important. Hopefully, along the way, we can find a small piece of his personality and the measure of the man. At any rate, he was an important figure, and you must know his story to know the history of modern African politics and culture.

The tip of Africa is home to some of the oldest human fossils that have been discovered by archaeologists and anthropologists. The United Nations considers it to be a World Heritage Site. The world is in agreement, the area now known as South Africa is likely to be the cradle of all civilization as we know it.

As such, the nation of South Africa is a great microcosm of the history of humanity itself. In the present day, the people of South Africa enjoy a multicultural, diverse society that is unrivaled in terms of the variety of cultures that can be found inside of it. To be South African is to be a member of the "Rainbow Nation" and a citizen of the 2nd most industrious nation in Africa.

However, along with an above-average economy, South Africa is home to great inequality. Poverty is an especially fierce foe on the tip of the continent. What is a growing problem in many western nations is a fiercely familiar enemy in South Africa.

Various tribes and collectives of people and pre-human ancestors have claimed ownership of the land throughout a period of about 3 million years. According to archaeologists, modern humans have existed in the area for around 170,000 years. But it seems the number is ever growing.

Eventually, it was conquered by the Bantu people and civilization began in earnest in that area with their mastery of iron and metal alloys. Sometime in the 15th century, it was discovered that there could be a sea route around the cape of Africa, the Cape of Good Hope.

This is only important to the story of Mandela in that his country began much the same way as many of the new world countries of the Americas. For many centuries, the ownership of the cape of

Africa was passed around by the various western powers. This created a stew of political and cultural boundaries and mergers that is, frankly, dizzying at times.

It became a land of slaves and owners. Once the Dutch, and then the British, had their say, the people of South Africa were as divided as they were various. To this day, there are groups of white people who believe they can trace their lineage back to a group of African Dutch — and harbor very racist views towards their native black African and foreign neighbors.

Mandela was born in 1918 at a time where the country was moving solidly away from British rule as the sun set on the old empire. During their rule, the country was widely segregated by racial bounds. The balance of power between the English-speaking whites and Afrikaners was not equal. By the time the Native's Land Act was passed in 1913, native Africans controlled under 10% of their home country.

Eventually, South Africa officially claimed its victory from the chains of colonialization in 1931 with the Statute of Westminster. However, it had been moving in a decidedly anti-British direction for some time. Even the white political bloc agreed that it was time for the country to take its fate into its own hands.

However, once World War II started, the country was split again. The natives wanted no part of the war between European powers and the English-speaking whites wanted to help their mother country. After the war, the party known as the National Party was elected to power. This would be the beginning of a system known as Apartheid.

The rule of the National Party would be defined by its essential racial qualities. They were white nationalists that wished to see their country become a place of segregation and a bulwark to what would be called miscegenation. At this point, Mandela was already a man and heavily involved in the political movement to allow rights to all people of South Africa.

Over the course of a couple of decades, the government became more and more hostile to dissenting opinions from any that were in opposition to apartheid. The policy was implemented under the guise of being something that would be beneficial to all the people of South Africa. However, it was obvious that the true intention was to provide an institutional apparatus to permanently place white men into power.

By 1961, the country had become a Republic and started to become a pariah on its own continent. Opposition to the political power of Apartheid spread across the world and the government didn't move an inch. Violence was, indeed, inevitable. What could simple men do against the power of a Republic?

Mandela became a part of several groups that stood in opposition to this, now entrenched, government. There was the Azanian People's Organization, the Pan-Africanist Congress, and Nelson's own African National Congress (or the ANC).

These organizations were both political and, eventually, violent in nature. However, it must be noted that these people were fighting a government that they rightly felt did not represent them.

They were oppressed far more viciously and over a much longer period than the American colonists that fought for their independence in the 18th and 19th century. It may be right to eschew violence in these situations, but it is hardly the right of an American or Frenchman to judge.

The government employed security forces and tried to squash the opposition at every turn, humanely or not. Guerilla tactics were soon the only resort left to the political organizations that wanted to oppose nationalist power and apartheid. The influence of these groups varied, with fights between opposition groups common.

However, the world had been moving away from racial politics, following the rise and fall of Hitler's Nazi Germany. Sanctions and international actions were taken against the National Party government. Still, they did not relent. By the 1970's, they had nuclear weapons and were a global force.

During their rise as a nuclear power, Mandela worked steadily as a political activist and professional rebel. There were many times when he had to hide or disguise himself to avoid the long arm of the law. He was charged with treason at one point but managed to avoid any permanent damage.

Then came that part of his life that everyone knows him for; as a part of a sting, Mandela was captured with another fellow activist. It would be revealed later that the information needed to capture Mandela came from none other than the C.I.A. who were afraid of his possible Communist sympathies.

Soon, there was another trial, and this time Mandela would be sentenced to life imprisonment. This was to the dismay of the prosecution, who had demanded the death penalty. Nonetheless, Mandela was transported to Robben Island Prison to serve a sentence for 18 years.

Life was brutal and he was under the command of exclusively white guards, some of which took out their own racial frustrations on the defenseless prisoner.

By the time the 1980's came around, the whole international climate around Mandela's imprisonment began to change. Ronald Reagan, the United States President, and Margaret Thatcher, the United Kingdom Prime Minister both supported the South African Nationalist on the grounds that the ANC was sympathetic to communism.

Thus, Mandela's prison sentence was continued and he was transported to another prison after his stay on Robben. It was here that Mandela would escape, but not through some grand scheme, after 27 years, the world Mandela lived in changed around him. After 27 years he was free.

Eventually, Mandela would win power for his people in the government and he would further enshrine the nation's turn towards a post-apartheid society. The nightmare was finally over for Mandela, in many ways though, the next challenge had just begun.

The next two decades brought about massive change for the nation of South Africa. It is a place of many tribulations from within and without. Poverty in South Africa increased for both the white and black segments of its population and it suffers from both xenophobia and economic hardships brought upon by a high immigration rate.

Again, it would appear the problems found in South Africa mirror those of the world, at large. But, it's time to take a step back and figure out how we got here--more specifically, it's time to discover the makeup of a man that has had a massive impact on human society across the globe. Who was the man, Nelson Mandela?

Early Life

Mandela was born the son of a chief and councilor for his village in 1918 South Africa. His early life was not the lap of luxury you might expect with that title. Though Mandela's great-grandfather was the king of all the Thembu people in the Eastern Cape Province, his side of the family was ineligible to be anything other than councilors and advisors.

Mandela barely knew his own father as it turned out. He was a polygamist and married four times in four different villages. All told, he had 4 sons and 9 daughters across the Eastern Cape.

His parents were illiterate and he spent much of his time working on the land with two of his sisters. Nelson Mandela, the most respected name in African politics in the modern era, began his working life as a cattle-boy. Such is the story of hardship and adversity in Nelson Mandela's life.

Mandela's tribe spoke Xhosa. The history of the tribe of Xhosa speaking people is a truly incredible odyssey that helps inform the tremendous instability that exists to this day.

There was, at one point, a war provided by the militaristic emperor, Shaka Zulu, that destabilized and very nearly depopulated a region in South Africa. It is estimated that 1-2 million people died there during a 30-year period in the 19th century.

Still, there has been persistent habitation by the Bantu people in the South African area for hundreds of years. Those that ended up speaking Xhosa, like Mandela's Thembu tribe, are the progeny of that ancient occupation.

However, once the Dutch and English immigrants had lived there for long enough, it became clear that they would fight for ownership of the area; as people are want to do — regardless of ancestral ownership.

Understandably, the Xhosa did not take the encroachment of the new inhabitants lightly. Many wars were had between the native Xhosa speaking people and the Boer tribes that found their roots in the Dutch.

100 years before the birth of Nelson Mandela, there was the Cape Frontier Wars located near the Cape Colony, the original Dutch colony in South Africa. The battles fought around the cape lasted on-and-off for about a century. Clearly, the effects of this war were felt for decades afterward. By the end of these conflicts, any independent Xhosa state was wiped out and replaced by the British.

As was stated earlier, the British were eventually ousted by the local inhabitants. But, for the most part, the rifts that caused the wars existed long after the last shot was fired on a battlefield.

The conflicts, from that point, mirror those that occurred during the period referred to as Manifest Destiny by the United States. Famine and death followed the Xhosa for many years.

Mandela's station was not of such despair, however. It was a very agrarian existence but safe from the horrors of pandemic and pestilence, largely. In fact, by most standards, idyllic might be the word for Qunu, his hometown.

From Mandela's memoir,

"Nature was our playground. The hills above Qunu were dotted with large smooth rocks which we transformed into our own rollercoaster. We sat on flat stones and slid down the face of the rocks. We did this until our backsides were so sore we could hardly sit down."

His homeland is still mostly rural and has few modern-day luxuries. It was there that he was bestowed his given name of Rolihlahla—or "troublemaker". His name would change depending on his location, Mandela being the English name given to him, and finally Madiba, his proper clan name. But, there was certainly some serendipity in his original naming.

He lived a very typical rural African life in Qunu, and the nearby villages of Mvezo and Mqekwzweni (where he went to school). Stick fighting was the game to play and most people lived in mud structures with floors made from anthill material.

Mandela would become known for his pride and competitive spirit. He was a ferocious fighter and a made a name for himself throughout town. A villager asked about Mandela tells a story form his younger days,

"When Madiba [Mandela's clan name] was a young boy, he was given his first pair of proper shoes to wear. But they were too large for him. He was so proud of them – he was a proud boy – but when he wore them through the village, all the girls laughed at him."

Mandela's father would die before he turned ten. That was when his life truly began to open up, as he put it, he felt that he had been "cut loose". Understandably, he didn't feel close enough to his father to be exceptionally sorrowful. After all, he was estranged from him for most of his childhood. Mandela felt like he was freed from the experience.

It was around this time that his mother sent him to a Methodist school where he was baptized and given his "Christian" name of Nelson Mandela by his Methodist instructors. He was a good student and quickly became a very serious and pious young boy.

Not to be completely immersed in Western Culture, Mandela was sent away to the "Great Place" in neighboring Mqhekezweni. It was there that he was adopted by a powerful local family. Again, he was much closer to his mother than his father, but he stills sees the experience in a positive light.

Mandela says that the time he spent there was as if he had spent it with his own family and the family of Chief Jongintaba treated him as their own.

Mandela began attending church even more and became a devout Methodist thanks to the Methodist mission school that was located nearby. Thankfully, he could learn both English and Xhosa there, solidifying a foundation of learning and self-improvement that would help him immensely during his imprisonment.

Mandela was torn when it came to how he felt about his home country. On one hand, he was present in his adopted father's court for all the political dealings that occurred in his realm — much of which was critical to the colonialists Mandela had come to rely on.

Yet, on the other hand, Mandela was grateful for the help with his education and other societal benefits that came with the imperial influences. This duality influenced him, in no small measure. When he tried to convert the disparate political groups opposed to apartheid, he was staunchly against looking down on whites that protested apartheid — something that was becoming common while he was imprisoned.

Mandela underwent the traditional circumcision ritual when he was 16 and became a man in the eyes of his village. It was then that he was given another name, "Dalibunga".

Mandela aspired to become a councilor to royalty, a profession that was common in his bloodline. So, he set off to yet another Methodist School to get his secondary education. He went to a school famous for having a large population of Thembu black Africans.

Mandela had previously been a bit of a square. He was heavily involved in the church and an attentive apprentice when it came to observing the political nature of his adopted father's position. So, it never really occurred to him that there might be a lighter side to life.

Thanks to the Clarkebury Methodist High School, Mandela was finally able to let go and come out of his shell. He even started to mix with women and became an avid gardener. He wasn't all green-thumb though, Mandela was an athlete as well— running and boxing at his next secondary school, Fort Beaufort.

It was at Fort Beaufort that his nature for acceptance was furthered. He came under the tutelage of a fellow Xhosa that broke with tradition and married into a rival Bantu tribe known as the Sotho. Mandela was inspired and made a friend of that tribe as well.

It was now that Mandela began to look further than the simple tribal squabbles that dominated politics and began to seriously consider a unified South Africa. It is truly inspiring to think that he had this dream so young and was able to work and live long enough to see it happen in his lifetime.

Nelson was an above average student and was accepted into the University of Fort Hare, a prestigious institution that was, again, segregated based on skin color. He studied humanity and language — including a brief foray into law that wound up helping him later in life when he studied law in prison.

It was here that he also met many friends that would come to be very important in the coming years, including Oliver Tambo. Tambo would be a hugely important figure in Mandela's life; he would lead the ANC during his prison term and was largely responsible for gathering international acclaim for Mandela.

Like many in the high society of South Africa, Mandela supported the war effort to help the British Isles during World War II. But, he was still given to bucking traditions and speaking truth to authority.

When he was a freshman in college he joined a group that staged a boycott to protest the quality of the food at the cafeteria. In an almost humorous replay of his political career, he was suspended from school for a time. Nelson never returned to University.

Instead, he returned home with his adopted brother. They both had a surprise waiting for them—a wife for each. Instead of being overjoyed at what their parents assuredly considered a gift, they were appalled. Apparently, it only took one year of college to get him off the concept entirely.

It was then that Mandela traveled to Johannesburg with his brother and began the next stage of his life. Gone were the days of idyllic countryside and moral certitude, Mandela was about to become wrapped up in one of the most incredible stories of political intrigue in the history of his country.

Johannesburg Runaway

For years, Mandela was putting off "becoming a man" fully until he could receive his education. Once most men were 16 in his culture, they would undergo a rite of initiation that included a circumcision ritual (likely extremely painful, he would speak about it later in life). After that, they were expected to set about finding work and growing a family, much like every other culture on the planet.

But, there was a new order for the Thembu people once the modern world intruded upon their customs. Now, Mandela, a well-to-do boy from the tribe, had all the skills and abilities to go to college and become a person of "great books and important papers" — as his clansmen put it.

However, life comes at you fast, and now, thanks to the controlling nature of his adopted father, he found himself in Johannesburg. He would have to become a man in a modern way, underneath the big city lights of the greatest and most conflicted city in South Africa.

He arrived in South Africa in April 1941 and his life was changed completely from that point on. His time in Johannesburg separated him in space and spirit from the village life that he had known for so many years. His early life was marked by learning and he was always especially interested in African history. But, the seclusion of rural life was never going to be enough for young Mandela.

Mandela had harbored aspirations that were majorly influenced by the time he spent in the court of his adopted family. He spent much of his time learning English and other languages so that he could be a court interpreter and work in the Civil service.

However, many people in his life noted that he would be an excellent lawyer. So, when he left for Johannesburg, Mandela's options opened up again. He would set out to work on finishing the degree that he started by taking correspondence courses from the University of South Africa. Mandela would need some help along the way, though.

So, through a mutual friend, Mandela met a man named Walter Sisulu, another transplant from Thembu village life. Sisulu had already been in Johannesburg and made quite a name for himself. Sisulu was also a member of the African National Congress and so the pieces began to fall into place for Mandela.

Sisulu ran a real estate business in Johannesburg and lived in a township known as Orlando. Sisulu had a larger-than-life personality and spent much of his early life working odd jobs, once leading a strike at a biscuit factory that he was soon fired from.

This was the theme for Mandela's next chapter. He was introduced to the world of

Capitalism on an international scale in Johannesburg. Mandela would also work in side-jobs in industries that were heavily exploitive, urging him to a more egalitarian perspective.

At the time, Communism was an influential force in South Africa. Despite what some might think about the ethics of Communism, it is definitely a move that makes sense. The forces of oppression for native Africans were staunch defenders of Capitalism.

The bad vibes between the Africans and their white peers reached such a point that some were vehemently opposed to fighting Hitler in WWII. The cultural lines were the strongest in that battle, but Mandela and his fellow ANC compatriots would see the stigma around Communism follow them throughout their struggle.

Mandela, himself, would end up eschewing Communism. He was a staunch Christian and Communism encouraged Atheism. He was also committed to the teachings Anton Lembede, someone who began to read in college. Lembede was enthusiastically supportive South African nationalism. This meant rejecting foreign doctrines like Communism. Mandela would, instead, focus on the ANC and his relationship with Sisulu.

Sisulu had connections that would be able to power Mandela to the life he dreamed of. The journey started with the firm known as Witken, Sidelsky & Eidelman. They were known throughout the city as being one of the only law firms that treated the Native African clientele equally.

Sisulu must have seen great promise in Mandela because he used the favor he amassed with the law firm to land Mandela a position as a clerk. He, at the same time, would pay for Mandela's tuition at the University of South Africa. Not only that, he ignored dire warnings about being associated with Mandela now that he had "abandoned" his post at The Great Place with his adopted family.

This problem would soon correct itself, however, and Mandela would meet his adopted father Jongintaba in Johannesburg during a visit. To Mandela, he was his greatest mentor and father figure.

Jongintaba saw that his protégé had created an influential and industrious life for himself and the relationship was mended quickly. He began to send Mandela an allowance and the two would find peace again. Unfortunately, Jongintaba died soon after and the allowance stopped.

Mandela went back to his hometown and spent some time collecting himself. He remembered how his father figure would listen to disparate ideas, even when he already disagreed with them. He knew that was how a leader became great and decided to spend his life emulating him.

African National Congress

Upon returning to Johannesburg, Mandela began to become more involved in politics. Sisulu was already recruiting for the African National Congress, with Mandela being one of his greatest recruitments. Members of the ANC had previously expressed concern that the future of the political movement was found in the young men who had interest in the nationalist movement.

Mandela and Sisulu meet a man named Oliver Tambo during the formulation of their next activist group. He had been a peer of Mandela's at Fort Hare Secondary School and was also interested in the ANC. The duo of Mandela and Tambo would work well together for decades. Tambo was the brains and Mandela took care of showmanship and persuasion.

So, Mandela, Sisulu, and Tambo created a Youth League for the African National Congress. The objective was simple; they would create a mechanism for members of the ANC to spread their ideologies to interested Africans. The Youth League accepted all Africans between 12-40. In a show of solidarity, they also accepted anybody from that age that "lived like and with Africans".

Their early tenets were simple and critical of the older leadership of the ANC that had begun before Mandela's birth. They believed that the ANC was too loosely regulated and wanted to create a more central and organized group. This effort was to be led by Anton Lembede, himself. What was lost on young Africans with the more "privileged" approach the old ANC took was revitalized by the Congressional Youth League's enthusiasm and ability.

Initially, their focus was on finding non-violent ways to improve the cause of African nationalism. The organization was far more defiant than its predecessor and regularly staged demonstrations of civil disobedience like boycotts and strikes.

Mandela had begun to act long before he took a leadership role with the CYL. In 1943, he participated in a bus boycott that was organized to combat rising fare prices, in an effort to support the more impoverished people in his area.

It was around the forming of the Congressional Youth League that Mandela entered into another kind of Union. He met a young woman named Evelyn Mase, who was also a member of the ANC when he was staying with Walter Sisulu. For a time after their marriage, Mandela found peace in working for the law firm during the day and being active with the political movement in his free time.

He was said to have enjoyed his domestic life very much. Once he found a place to live, he invited members of his extended family to stay with him and he was able to start a small family of his own. However, it was obvious that Mandela would not be content with his current station. Once he finished his clerkship with the firm, he began immediately securing a spot at the university full time, with the help of public grants.

However, there would be no time for Mandela and his friends to rest on their laurels. As quickly and brilliantly had the reign of Anton Lembede began, so did his presidency come to an end. In 1947, at just 33 years of age, Anton Lembede died.

There was an immediate power vacuum in the CYL. Lembede was eventually succeeded by a more moderate figure. Later that year the ANC would face a rift when Mandela publicly supported an act that would have expelled Communists from the ANC.

Mandela, following Lembede's teachings, felt that it was wrong to accept a foreign ideology into their platform.

Unfortunately for the members of the youth branch of the ANC, as well as all Africans in the region, something truly terrible was about to begin in South Africa. At a time when other major powers of the world were experiencing a more egalitarian cultural shift in the wake of WWII, South Africa was heading in a heavily racist direction.

Apartheid

There's so much in the public consciousness when it comes to apartheid. For many in the western world, it is seen as a moment in time that resembled the post-civil war American conflict over racial injustice. To others closer to the event, it was a confluence of actions and feelings that were truly unique. Therefore, it is everyone's best interest to examine the sources behind one of history's most oppressive cultural regimes.

For a very long time, the government of South Africa was dominated by the power of white politics. Although it was a land with a majority of native Africans, the Dutch and then the English would control the government and laws of the land for the entire existence of what was a de facto "colony".

Even after the government distanced itself from the rule of the British over time, the decision to do so was still made by white South Africans who had consolidated power as the British influence waned.

Thus, freed from any moral constraints imposed by the already condescending British, the route of the country took a decidedly racial turn. Apartheid means "separateness" and has much in common with segregation. However, American segregation included (however limited) voting rights for black citizens and permitted (however dangerous) interracial marriages at a federal level.

Of course, despite their differences, the racial conflicts of the Americas and Africa have one very important aspect in common: slavery. So, in 1833, when the United Kingdom passed its Slavery Abolition Act, there was a good deal of trouble caused by the white men in power who still wanted to use the African population as slaves.

That's something important to remember: Apartheid is not a sudden display of racial issues in South Africa. Ever since the passing of the Slavery Abolition Act, legislation was in constant motion to keep the African population in the pocket of white former slaveholders.

Laws were passed immediately to simply remove the designation of a slave from the

African Xhosa population and to keep the flow of cheap, unskilled labor into South Africa. Along with the exploitation, came the cultural battles. The government feared any interracial unions amongst its people and there was much longstanding legislation to keep the two populations apart, no matter how much the individuals wanted to be together.

By the beginning of the 20th century, Jim Crowe-type laws were put into effect nationally. The Franchise and Ballot Act of 1892 limited black voting rights to only wealthy members of society, of which there were few African participants. What follows that is a laundry list of legislative injustices that mirrors only that of the worst KKK visions for Africans.

In order, blacks were not permitted to own large tracts of land (that would run afoul of the Franchise and Ballot Act if it was possible for Africans to build wealth). The government then eliminated their right to vote entirely and instituted rules for requiring blacks to stay in certain areas and created a "Pass" system that forced Blacks into living in certain areas. Before Mandela was even born, the Native Land Act was passed that forbid blacks from purchasing land that was not on certain reserves.

After the government declared itself independent from Britain, there was a power struggle amongst the white political forces, still, the Africans benefitted from no good shakes from the national institutions. Further laws were passed that removed any African participation in their parliament and the voter rolls were completely purged of all black voting power.

By the time Mandela was active in the ANC, the world was embroiled in WWII and South Africa faced a decision on the direction the country would go. The government was, then, run by the United Party. They began to soften some of the regulations that kept Africans from participating in society.

However, there was a blowback from the South African political elite and a commission was instituted to decide if integration was possible. The findings were less than helpful for the state of Africans in South Africa.

Then, the tides turned for the worst, if that was possible. The election of 1948 in South Africa was the beginning of one of the worst episodes of segregation the world had ever seen. Previously, most of the political and social efforts to derail black enfranchisement and economic power were allowed to exist socially and without codified law.

Then, in 1948, the National party was elected to power under the explicit mandate of establishing racial power boundaries and to implement ever more strict segregation. Interestingly, the rhetoric that was established by the National Party was based on the idea that softening racial regulations were the result of foreign influences from western liberal thinking.

It becomes clear, that the impetus behind both the ANC and the National Party were based on nationalism. It is wise to note that fervent nationalism at the risk of other parties that you consider "non-national" can be used as a force of ultimate evil as well. Populism gives and takes away.

Much of the power that was given to the National party is found in the ancestrally Dutch populations (these days they are referred to as Boers and their story continues to be racially charged and fascinating) that were given to anger towards both Africans (racially and economically) and towards the more privileged English-speaking whites.

Thus, the National Party came to power and their principal was to segregate their population into 13 distinct racial groups. From that point forward, Africans and other races deemed "colored" by the government, were forced to live in certain townships and operate their lives based on strictly racial terms.

Laws were passed that forced individuals to carry ID cards that verified their identity as a part of a racial group. If your family was mixed, a commission would determine what race each person belonged to — sometimes separating family groups based off of color lines that they, themselves, never observed.

Acts were soon passed that created "reservations" for non-whites that were later used as a justification for forced removal. Then, of course, was the federal ban on interracial marriages and, even further, legislation that made it illegal to even have sexual relations with those of a different race.

Of course, something to note here is that, despite the rhetoric that promised a more prosperous nation under apartheid, it typically just resulting in worse living conditions for non-whites. Rarely would a white person be arrested for relations with a non-white, but the punishments for interracial relationships were swift and sever for black Africans. Eventually it became only blacks that were required to carry ID's indicating their race.

By the mid-50, segregation of schools, public services, restrooms, and even public spaces was commonplace and accepted. The National Party was allowed to stay in power throughout this time by disenfranchising "colored" voters any chance they had. The government became a de facto arm for racists throughout the country.

This plunge into extreme racial politics follows the same guidelines established in the slavery South and Hitler's Germany. Mandela and his ANC family were dismayed, but not surprised. To them, their work had just begun — and it was far, far from over.

Fighting Apartheid and the Trial of 1956

In direct opposition to apartheid, the ANC began plans to induct full citizenship for every African in South Africa in 1949. The Congressional Youth League made its mark on the ANC and their objectives changed quickly from a Booker T. Washington type of approach (read: appeasement) to civil disobedience in the thread of Martin Luther King (however anachronistic).

They demanded compulsory education for the children of South Africa, unions, and redistribution of land that would include reparations for previous legislation that took land away from Africans. Obviously, due to disenfranchisement, the tides of politics were headed in the opposite direction — limiting the ANC to working outside of the legislature and laws. Thus, began Mandela's long and terrible relationship with authorities in South Africa.

Mandela, along with Sisulu and Tambo, began to push the ANC towards a more radical path. They began to see themselves as revolutionaries. Mandela soon abandoned his studies at the University, failing his final courses over three different years. He was not given a degree and became completely committed to politics and defiance.

Sisulu and Tambo became executive officials of the group once the leadership splintered over how radical their tactics should be. Soon, Mandela was also asked to be on the council. His prophetic rise began when, later that same year, he was elected as the national president of the Congressional Youth League arm of the ANC—his and Sisulu's pet project.

A change was soon to occur in Mandela's mind. Once Lembede was gone from the power structure, the ANC began to debate adding other races into their ranks. As Lembede would have wanted, Mandela resisted the idea. He was convinced that a successful movement was hinged on the fact that it was an African national movement.

He was outvoted multiple times, and the audacity of his allies to include other races into their liberation efforts changed his mind over the years. At the same time, this opened his mind up to Communism, which (again despite personal opinions about its efficacy) would run him afoul of the government in new and interesting ways.

As a form of protest prohibition, the National Party government passed laws limiting the ability for citizens to participate in organized worker protests, which was a popular ANC tactic. Thus, Mandela and the ANC was lumped in with Communism. To the government, it was easy to pass off demonstrations to their Western allies as "communist". That left them plenty of political ability to suppress the African national movement on the basis of fighting Communism.

However, the African National Congress was not dissuaded from their cause. With every protest they launched, their numbers grew. After Mandela held a nonviolent resistance movement known as the "Defiance" campaign, their registered members began to multiply — in a few years they increased their membership 5-fold.

This new popularity also launched the political career of Nelson Mandela. He was seen as the face of these new movements and was publicly arrested for multiple protests. The National Party government responded with more arrests and eventually the Public Safety Act of 1953, or more plainly, martial law.

It was under these new Draconian laws that Mandela was arrested in 1952 under the guise of suppressing communism, effectively ending his reign as president of the ANC. The terms of his probation precluded Mandela from meeting with more than one person at a time. It soon became tradition to read Mandela speeches at rallies he couldn't be present at.

Mandela and the executives at the ANC expected that they would soon be banned altogether. So, Mandela created the "M-Plan" that established a "cell" structure for the ANC that relied on the central leadership for instruction. This is setup is much more like a liberation group (including terrorist organizations). It is a way to project power with an organization without creating easy-to-attack locations.

Mandela, himself, was finally able to finish the certifications that would allow him to become a lawyer. He and Tambo opened up a law firm that catered specifically to blacks that had legal grievances. At the time, they were the only African law firm in South Africa, a truly impressive feat. He became a much-loved member of his community thanks to his work against police brutality.

Meanwhile, his family life was falling apart as he spent most of his time working for political motivations. With most of his time spent at the office, allegations of adultery started to surface and he lost the affection of his wife and adopted mother. To make matters worse, his law firm was forcibly relocated to a remote part of town, nearly decimating his client base.

The ANC leadership, knowing that their protests were being brutally squashed at every turn, decided that it was time to reorganize politically and, if necessary, militarily. They joined together with several other anti-apartheid groups to create the "Freedom Charter". This outlined what life would be like after the National Party government was ousted.

It included: free mixing of races, a democratic form of government, and the nationalization of industries in the country. Mandela was unable to make any waves with the Freedom Charter, as the police shut down the meeting of over 3000 members. However, the meaning of the Freedom Charter persisted:

"We, the people of South Africa, declare for all our country and the world to know: That South Africa belongs to all who live in it, black and white, and that no government can justly claim authority unless it is based on the will of the people."

Over the next couple of years, Mandela would divorce, remarry, and receive 3 more bans from public appearances — including a 5-year ban from Johannesburg. Mandela took no heed of the ban and continued to work for the ANC.

The culmination of these events was Mandela's arrest in 1956. He and the executive bloc of the ANC were arrested for "high treason" and forced into a public trial. The protests that occurred as a result of the arrests were massive and they were granted bail. Over the next four years, Mandela and his defense stated their case against stacked odds.

The justice system in South Africa must have maintained a sense of jurisprudence throughout the madness, and the three National Party judges that presided over the case were dismissed after an appeal by the defense. The case began to turn for their side.

However, everything changed after the Sharpeville Massacre. The ANC joined together with a racially charged group that accepted only blacks, known as the Pan-Africanist Congress. They staged a joint protest to burn their passes (the ones they were obligated to carry and that stated their government prescribed race) and created a mass demonstration movement across the nation.

In Sharpeville, the protests grew in size until the police snapped. Armed militia fired upon a crowd of its own citizens, killing 69 people in the process. The world, and the nation of South Africa, was rocked. Mandela, previously withholding of his status in the general society, burned his pass in solidarity. Then, the riots began across the entirety of South Africa.

With the country falling apart due to its failed policies, the government doubled down. Martial law was, again, enforced. Both the ANC and the Pan-Africanist Congress (PAC) were banned organizations and Mandela and company were again arrested.

This time, as a precursor of things to come, Mandela was imprisoned with his compatriots in a dilapidated local prison for 6 months. His trial would continue, regardless of the circumstances, infuriating his defense. However, knowing their hand was being forced by the people, the trial ended in a not guilty verdict. Mandela was freed for the first time.

However, things had changed permanently on the other side of the prison walls. Mandela could no longer safely travel openly in public. The government considered the trial an embarrassment after its claims of high treason. They were waiting for any chance they could get to bring him in for good.

So, Mandela began a life of deceit and disguise. He would dress as a chauffeur and travel around the country, organizing protests. He would receive warrants for his arrest as a result. Mandela's politics of freedom and racial equality was officially illegal in the country of South Africa.

The riots continued for the duration of the early 60's and eventually Mandela and the

ANC decided to take action. Knowing that violence was already occurring and they could do nothing to stop it, short of endorsing the government, the ANC decided to turn the violence into directed military action.

Again, it's easy to look at that decision and see it as an overreaction from the comfort of a sofa. However, their countrymen were being murdered in the streets and people were being killed either way. They decided to harness the anger for a long-term goal, not unlike other revolutions that the western world has been shaped by.

Mandela was inspired by the concurrent revolution in Cuba by Fidel Castro and decided to create a military wing of the

ANC, known as Umkhonto we Sizwe, translated as Spear of the Nation. The organization, known as MK, was not to be officially connected to the ANC, but was affiliated regardless.

The initial membership simply consisted of Mandela and the various Communist-connected affiliates that were harboring Mandela. If there was a time that Mandela could be considered a Communist was during this period in the early-60. Although it was not necessarily accepted throughout the world, Communism (and Castro) was considered to be a viable option.

Mandela had been pushed to his own personal extremes by the radical, racial legislation of the National Party. So, the MK decided to enact a campaign of sabotage. They didn't want to engage in open warfare, instead they chose to bomb public installations like power plants and telephone lines. In 1961, they declared that they were active when they bombed over 57 locations on a single day.

Mandela was prepared to begin engaging in guerrilla warfare as the situation progressed. He toured states that were sympathetic to the plight of the South African struggle and began learning military tactics in place of his previous political and military training.

Before history could find out if that was a mistake, Mandela was arrested one final time. He, and another MK member, was detained on the orders of the South African government. But it was the order of another government that had the most pronounced effect.

Not many knew at the time, but according to later revelations that have been corroborated, it turns out that the American Central Intelligence Agency was responsible for locating Mandela and giving the information directly to the South African government. Fighting Communism had butted up against the plight of non-white peoples once again. This time, it could have meant death for one of the world's most important figures.

Still, Mandela, again, received charges that were unlikely to stick. His initial case only included charges of inciting strikes and leaving the country without permission. However, unluckily for Mandela, an MK base was raided during the proceedings for his first trial. The raid uncovered information that linked both Mandela and the MK to violent acts of sabotage throughout the country. This time was different.

The prosecution had teeth this time and more proof than they ever had before. Fearing another overreach, the prosecution did not ask for treason charges, rather they raised accusations of conspiracy and sabotage. These charges were much easier to prove, with one small caveat for the government who wanted Mandela dead; they did not typically lead to death sentences.

Mandela took this time to express his true outrage to the larger, worldwide audience and delivered a 3-hour speech entitled "I Am Prepared to Die", it ended with this statement of defiance:

Children wander about the streets of the townships because they have no schools to go to, or no money to enable them to go to school, or no parents at home to see that they go to school, because both parents (if there be two) have to work to keep the family alive. This leads to a breakdown in moral standards, to an alarming rise in illegitimacy, and to growing violence which erupts not only politically, but everywhere. Life in the townships is dangerous. There is not a day that goes by without somebody being stabbed or assaulted. And violence is carried out of the townships in the white living areas. People are afraid to walk alone in the streets after dark. Housebreakings and robberies are increasing, despite the fact that the death sentence can now be imposed for such offences. Death sentences cannot cure the festering sore.

Africans want to be paid a living wage. Africans want to perform work which they are capable of doing, and not work which the Government declares them to be capable of. Africans want to be allowed to live where they obtain work, and not be endorsed out of an area because they were not born there. Africans want to be allowed to own land in places where they work, and not to be obliged to live in rented houses which they can never call their own. Africans want to be part of the general population, and not confined to living in their own ghettoes. African men want to have their wives and children to live with them where they work, and not be forced into an unnatural existence in men's hostels. African women want to be with their menfolk and not be left permanently widowed in the Reserves. Africans want to be allowed out after eleven o'clock at night and not to be confined to their rooms like little children. Africans want to be allowed to travel in their own country and to seek work where they want to and not where the Labor Bureau tells them to. Africans want a just share in the whole of South Africa; they want security and a stake in society.

Above all, we want equal political rights, because without them our disabilities will be permanent. I know this sounds revolutionary to the whites in this country, because the majority of voters will be Africans. This makes the white man fear democracy.

But this fear cannot be allowed to stand in the way of the only solution which will guarantee racial harmony and freedom for all. It is not true that the enfranchisement of all will result in racial domination. Political division, based on color, is entirely artificial and, when it disappears, so will the domination of one color group by another. The ANC has spent half a century fighting against racialism. When it triumphs, it will not change that policy.

This then is what the ANC is fighting. Their struggle is a truly national one. It is a struggle of the African people, inspired by their own suffering and their own experience. It is a struggle for the right to live.

I have fought against white domination, and I have fought against black domination. I have cherished the ideal of a democratic and free society in which all persons will live together in harmony and with equal opportunities. It is an ideal which I hope to live for and to see realized. But if it needs be, it is an ideal for which I am prepared to die."

Mandela was sentenced to life in prison, along with 2 of his compatriots. The United

Nations demanded his immediate release. The largest student union organization in Europe voted Mandela in as its president, symbolically. There was a new tide in the world. South Africa could no longer hide from the actions of its racist minority. Although, for Mandela, this was no victory—he could only imagine the horrors he was soon to face. But he would not take the punishment lying down.

Prison Life

"We were awakened at 5:30 each morning by the night warder, who clanged a brass bell at the head of our corridor and yelled, "Word wakker! Staan op!" (Wake up! Get up!) I have always been an early riser and this hour was not a burden to me. Although we were roused at 5:30, we were not let out of our cells until 6:45, by which time we were meant to have cleaned our cells and rolled up our mats and blankets. We had no running water in our cells and instead of toilets had iron sanitary buckets known as "ballies." The ballies had a diameter of ten inches and a concave porcelain lid on the top that could contain water. The water in this lid was meant to be used for shaving and to clean our hands and faces."

Gone was Mandela's neat, clean home life. Even as a member of an oppressed race, Mandela had always enjoyed an elevated role. After all, he had been the brightest and most charismatic. But, the time of privilege was over for him. He was interred at Robben Island prison and discovered quickly that prison life was just as racially divided as his life had been on the outside.

The African inmates were given the worst rations and treated horribly by the white jailers. Even among Indians and non-Africans, the place of the African was at the bottom again. Conditions weren't ideal in the first place, with inhumane treatments that would make Alcatraz look tame in comparison.

Mandela's cell was 8' x 7' and was essentially bare besides the latrine bucket they were responsible for cleaning. The bed was straw and the floors cold. He was isolated and could not speak to his fellow prisoners. Food was limited to nutrient powder and various bits of rough corn. The rations were so meager that the prisoners took to saving up their powder so that they could eat one full serving every now and then. They even served coffee — except it wasn't coffee, it was burnt-to-a-crisp corn that was ground into a powder.

The prisoners spent their days breaking up stones for the local quarry and eventually went about working with limestone. Mandela was forbidden to wear any eye protection and the formidable glare from the limestone partially blinded him for life. When they weren't working themselves to nubs, the prisoners would do everything they could to avoid contact with the more violent wardens. A misstep could mean a beating.

Mandela would develop many of his political skills that would go on to serve him well in the years to come during his time in prison. He understood that, in his position, it was in his best interest to develop good relationships with the "Warders" or jailers of his section. He stated in his memoirs:

"We had one warder at the quarry who seemed particularly hostile to us. This was troublesome, for at the quarry we would hold discussions among ourselves, and a warder who did not permit us to talk was a great hindrance. I asked a certain comrade to befriend this fellow so that he would not interrupt our talks. The warder was quite crude, but he soon began to relax a bit around this one prisoner. One day, the warder asked this comrade for his jacket so that he could lay it on the grass and sit on it. Even though I knew it went against the comrade's grain, I nodded to him to do it.

A few days later, we were having our lunch under the shed when this warder wandered over. The warder had an extra sandwich, and he threw it on the grass near us and said, "Here." That was his way of showing friendship.

The strategy worked, for this warder became less wary around us. He even began to ask questions about the ANC."

Such was the power of Mandela's diplomacy. He was able to be a political leader even in prison. It was certainly a time in which he truly had to learn to use the tools available to him. But, he was able to eventually make progress with the prison system.

However, he was still considered dangerous. He had the lowest level of clearance possible for a prisoner and was only allowed one 30 minute visit every six months. He was also only allowed one letter during this same time period. This meant that Mandela was to

be left completely separate from the world —
if they were to have their way.

Mandela, however, had different plans. He
knew the power of hope and was never
completely defeated. He spent many stays in
solitary confinement for simply carrying
nicked news clippings that he would show
to his fellow political prisoners. Eventually,
he would begin a correspondence degree
program again to get his law degree from a
prestigious university instead of his simple
certifications.

With the help of his ANC fellows, Mandela
and his group was able to gather support
quickly throughout the prison. They would
spend their days discussing politics and
philosophy, hoping to improve themselves

with every step along the way. Mandela was personally expanding was his studies to more varied sources. He even spent some time studying Islam, despite his Christian upbringing.

Perhaps the most important step he took was learning the language of the warders in his prison. He took it upon himself to convert every person he could find. In some ways, Mandela was finding his dream of being an interpreter come true — just in the very last place he would ever have imagined.

Tragedy would seem to come from every angle during this time. Both Mandela's mother and firstborn son passed away during his time there. He was forced to stay away from both funerals. The emotional fortitude that it takes to be able to even function after such blows is incredible. But, his external conditions were possibly worse than any inner turmoil.

Nothing could heal the damage done by losing loved one, but Mandela was able to affect his prison conditions in a positive way through very limited activism. Prison conditions began to improve, though slowly. When a more brutal commanding officer was hired for the post, Mandela was able to petition a judge to remove him. He was replaced with a man of a much more generous nature.

After some time, Mandela's prisoner status was changed to the most unrestrictive version. He was able to change his station by long term habits that endeared himself to the warders. He began to make friends out of the men who watched him. His supporters in the prison would come to revere him for his ability to accept pain and injustice and turn it into productive action.

Said a fellow political prisoner about Mandela:

"I was only 26 when I went to the island. We were really a hardline sort ... we just thought, 'Look, bugger these chaps, we are going to give them hell, etc.' without thinking that they could give us hell, you see. Then Nelson made the point to us one day saying, 'Look, you chaps shouldn't have any illusions about how long you are going to be here. In all probability, you are going to sit out the entire period.' Because we had been blithely talking about a two-year stay and then we will be liberated and all the rest of it. Those are the illusions of youth, and also of revolutionaries, generally.

So that set us thinking, because his point in telling us that was that--instead of kicking against the pricks ... let's spend some time strategizing. Let's see how we can transform the situation on the island. That really set me thinking, that instead of being reactive all the time, we could begin to be proactive. We could begin to create a new paradigm ... within which to restructure our existence on the island. That was one of the really important moments where he won me over. I don't think it was a question of wooing incidentally. It was just a pure, human almost fatherly touch that he had, and which he has."

It was through the actions of Mandela that the prisoners were able to win some of their rights back. They backbreaking labor was relented, they began to allow prisoners to talk to each other, and the warders even lifted the ban on smoking. The prison population, as a whole, began to spend its time in the library and rarely fought amongst themselves. Over time, the warders would be swayed to a form of begrudging respect.

Outside, the situation had not improved. The "Black Consciousness Movement" replaced the power the ANC had. It was almost a strictly military movement, putting its members in direct opposition to Mandela.

Their movement was limping after the Soweto Uprising, a demonstration by African school children numbering in the tens of thousands. 170+ children were murdered in the streets with some estimates reaching up to 700 deaths. After that, the government cracked down on the Black Consciousness Movement in a very serious way.

Thus, new recruits were being let into Robben Island with regularity. Mandela would have seen them as recruits, anyway. He set about convincing them to abandon their methods of violence, now wholly convinced that true victory over apartheid would have to come from changing people's hearts.

Time would continue to pass and soon enough Mandela was in his 60's. The world, in a strange show of compassion, had not forgotten his plight. He was increasing in popularity again — even though both the U.S. and U.K. governments still considered him a threat because of his former ties to Communism.

When he turned 60, he had been in prison for 14 years and was still just barely over halfway through what would become his full prison term. 4 years after his 60th birthday, he was transferred to Pollsmoor Prison along with Walter Sisulu. Mandela was sure that he was being targeted for removal because of the effect he was having on the younger prisoners.

Regardless, Mandela seemed to enjoy his time spent at Pollsmoor, at least in comparison to the conditions at Robben Island. Still, Mandela felt that he was doing something more meaningful when he was teaching the young activist prisoners.

By the 1980's, South Africa was falling apart. Mandela's support was skyrocketing across the world. Multinational industries began to pull their finances out of South Africa for fear of being mixed in with the very unpopular government. Even the U.K. began to withdraw their support for apartheid. Still, the National Party government would not relinquish its hold. It had transformed into something else entirely, a dictatorship bent on spreading its hateful teachings — even if it meant a civil war.

However, the racist government offered Mandela his freedom, in a shocking change of course, during the winter of 1985. The pressure was building and the National Party leadership tried to win an easy political victory by allowing Mandela to be free…as long as he condemned any violent revolutionaries from the newly-revived, but still banned, ANC.

Mandela replied, simply, "Only free men can negotiate. A prisoner cannot enter into contracts."

Over the next few years, the ANC would launch attacks numbering in the hundreds. Vigilante groups began to involve themselves, similar to the KKK in America. The government offered him another deal, this time claiming to unban the ANC, as long as he would renounce communism and (also!) majority rule.

Mandela again refused, not unless the government was willing to renounce its violent ways as well. This would be seen as an embarrassment by the National Party and it refused, as well.

Mandela would fall ill at Pollsmoor and was subsequently moved to a residence at a much better prison. He was allowed home cooked meals and plenty of time and resources to final, officially, earn his Bachelor degree in Law.

Not long after, a new president was elected to lead the National Party government by the name of F.W. de Klerk. He was the first president, since before the beginning of apartheid that believed the separation to be unsustainable. Surely this was obvious, as South Africa's standing in the world had dipped considerably.

On February 11th, 1990, the government officially announced that Mandela's unconditional release and rescinding the ban on the ANC. Mandela would leave prison and live with Desmond Tutu — soon he would

Give a speech to over 100,000 South Africans in Johannesburg.

Death of Apartheid, Presidency, and Legacy

Mandela was free and the ANC had legal status again. Not since before 1948 had Mandela and his supporters experienced such open and civil conditions. He went about the job of traveling the world and spreading his message. Apartheid, he believed, would not be achieved without international help.

Several benefit concerts were planned and held in his honor, with his fans soon numbering into the millions. Mandela's fame began to engulf the conversation. The fall of apartheid seemed likely, especially after the Berlin wall came down. Mandela was close to his goal.

He returned home to reform the ANC. He believed that it needed to return to a more organized and political organization. Oliver Tambo had been leading the organization throughout Mandela's prison sentence. Tambo had been responsible for much of the popularity that Mandela now enjoyed when he led several "Free Mandela" campaigns throughout the world.

Now, Nelson was to replace him (he was sick and welcomed the change) and lead the charge into the new political reality. The first step was to reduce violence throughout the country and Mandela was able to achieve that through negotiation. Just like he told his fellow prisoners in Robben Island, apartheid was to be conquered not on the battlefield but at the negotiation table — surely a thought that would have seemed insane only years before.

However, the work was not over yet. Long, numerous talks would take place between Mandela and President De Klerk over a couple of years. Mistrust was building between them and, when a peace accord served to do nothing more than pause the violence, Mandela marched on the capital in the largest mass demonstration in South Africa's history.

Despite the progress, the streets had become ever more dangerous. Now, there was infighting amongst African groups that disagreed on the way in which apartheid should be dismantled. There were thousands of deaths before any of this was resolved.

Still, Mandela and De Klerk continued to negotiate and were able to put together a "coalition government of national unity" that would be multiracial. Mandela made some concessions that angered his supporters, but he stood pat. Soon there would be an election in which all races could participate. Remembering his "I Am Prepared to Die" speech will recall his ultimate desire to have political enfranchisement, to show the true power of democracy.

South Africa would reform into 9 provinces and create a constitution based off the U.S. model. Mandela and De Klerk would receive a joint Nobel Peace Prize for this triumph of government. In 1994 the election was held that would forever change South Africa. It was not pretty, but Democracy never is.

Mandela and the ANC won a near supermajority — though the races were tainted by sabotage and fraud, Mandela himself admitted as much.

For the next five years, Mandela would be the president of South Africa. It took only 4 years for Mandela to go from prisoner to president. His ascent became a truly remarkable story that inspired millions around the world. In particular, the African American community would revere him as hero to look up to in their struggle for equality. A billion people would watch his inauguration.

Mandela ruled as Jongintaba ruled. He didn't allow his own opinions to affect his ability to listen to others. His moderation and kindness to all was his primary attribute. Though, he learned that there would always be someone who did not appreciate his evenhandedness.

His government was notable for its efforts to reconcile the racial issues that had dominated the politics of South Africa for so long. He did not wish to see his country lose money and influence because white investors were afraid to become involved. He met with important figures from the previous apartheid regime and attempted to mend relations with all that would listen.

In 1995, he would present the Rugby World Cup to the South African team composed of white Afrikaners. De Klerk would say of the move, "Mandela won the hearts of millions of white rugby fans." This moment would later be immortalized in the popular American film, Invictus.

He, also, established a commission to look into any atrocities committed by both the National Party and the ANC during apartheid — headed by none other than Bishop Desmond Tutu. However, South Africa had much more pressing issues to consider.

Facing 33% unemployment and a huge disparity between the communities of whites and blacks, the deck was already stacked against Mandela. However, by the end of his reign 3 million more people had telephone communication and more than 1.5 million children were brought into the compulsory education system. 3 million people were housed, 2 million were connected to electricity, and 3 million finally had access to public water services.

In 1999, Mandela retired. He left behind a solid constitution created during his rule and continued to support humanitarian efforts as a private citizen.

In 2013, Mandela died in his home of a respiratory illness. His legacy would be that of the father of the nation that we now know to be South Africa. He will be forever known as a figure of great human kindness and compassion.

But, Mandela was a lifelong defender of democracy and went to great lengths to provide that for the nation of people he represented. It might have been easy for him to have simply succumbed to prejudice and accept the same hate that was levied to him on a daily basis. Instead, he stood for the integration of all races in South Africa. He created what he liked to call, "a great rainbow nation".

The true cost of what Mandela experienced is unknowable. For every story that was told about his prison life, there are probably 10 that no one will ever hear about. For every second he spent in prison, there were years and years of strife and humiliation brought upon him by apartheid, even when he was free.

There is much to be criticized when it comes to Mandela's decisions over the years, but the truth is, the world is not an easy to understand place. By the standards of a normal human, Mandela went above and beyond his own limits — simply to protect the rights of others. For that alone, he will be remembered by the world as a great figure.

However, his greatest legacy lives on in the hearts and souls of the youth of South Africa. No longer are generations of men born without a future. Mandela often told the story of his circumcision; it began traditionally, but was stopped suddenly by the lament of the chief who was to speak at the event.

He cried in front of the group of boys as he realized that, although they were now men, they could never have much of a future in South Africa. He feared their lives would be lived in vain, performing menial chores for the white man.

Nelson Mandela refused that fate. He never forgot that moment and the world is a better place for it.

CPSIA information can be obtained
at www.ICGtesting.com
Printed in the USA
BVHW031456020520
579082BV00001B/200